HOW TO ACHIEVE TRUE FINANCIAL FREEDOM

INDEX

Chapter 1: What Financial Freedom Means

Chapter 2: Realities of Financial Independence

Chapter 3: Begin Your Journey to Financial Freedom

Chapter 4: Tips to Ensure a Successful Financial Independence Plan

Chapter 5: Working Toward Financial Independence

Chapter 6: New trends towards financial management

Chapter 7: Money Matters

Chapter 8: Distinguishing Between Wants and Needs in Life to Achieve Financial Freedom

Chapter 9: Organizing Your Debt for Financial Freedom

Chapter 10: Six Ways to Teach Children about Money and Financial Markets

Chapter 11: Financial Independence for seniors

Chapter 12: Financial Independence and Retirement Planning

Chapter 13: Freedom Has a Price

Chapter 14: Setting Goals for Financial Independence

Chapter 1: What Financial Freedom Means

In the 21st century, the concepts of time and money are being redefined. "Financial Freedom", is a term that has gained a lot of importance in the changing financial scenario.

"Financial Freedom" means the freedom from ongoing financial responsibilities through planned management and asset allocation. It frees a person from a strenuous job by giving them a stable source of income for life.

One should not think that a debt-free person

is also debt-free. However, their prudent asset management ensures that their debts do not become a burden, but only a part of their overhead. In this way, your debts do not stand in the way of your long-term financial goals.

Financial freedom cannot be equated with being rich. It should not be forgotten that excess wealth requires constant supervision. In the long run, a rich man's obligations do not make him "financially free" in the true sense. Thus, financial freedom can be defined as a lifestyle that mixes expenses and income according to individual preference. This makes "financial freedom" more possible and convenient.

Financial freedom is freedom of time

"Time is money," is the general belief in the professional world. This attitude leaves no room for free time. However, financial freedom has changed this concept of work by allowing a person to enjoy leisure without hindering their stable income in any way. The whole concept of "financial freedom" is based on assets and investments that are combined over time to generate money. It takes care of regular expenses and leaves a person with time and money in their hands. A financially independent person is free from the clutches of routine time for money.

Achieving Financial Freedom

To understand "financial freedom" you have

to get away from the traditional concepts of income and expenses.

We have been taught that timely work makes money. Financial freedom" is opposed to this concept of exchanging time for money and letting money work for us. However, despite this advantage many professionals find it difficult to work without a fixed routine.

Therefore, to achieve financial freedom one needs to change their old mentalities and develop a new attitude to making money. One must realize that money is simply the means to an end.

One must also remember that a person cannot be judged by the money he possesses. Unless these misconceptions are cleared up, the purpose of financial freedom will be defeated since satisfaction is the key word for financial freedom.

Similarly, one must also get rid of the negative attitude toward earning money. While excessive demand for wealth makes a healthy relationship with finances difficult, a healthy perception of money is necessary to maintain an excessive balance. Remember that one earns money to achieve ends and therefore it is healthy and normal to earn money as long as one feels an ethical need to do so.

In the end, it can be said that financial freedom is the state of mind that works towards development through a process of self-liberation.

Chapter 2: Realities of Financial Independence

Independence is a state of being that every living being strives to attain, and maintain forever. From the moment a child sets foot in school, he is made to understand that the knowledge he acquires from this point on is for him to make use of his intelligence, to shape his own future.

When one lives with one's parents, one tends to take many things for granted. Once you start earning a living, you are faced with two diabolical aspects: financial independence and responsibility.

Making money is not enough. Many factors arise when one (sometimes arrogantly) decides to separate from the family and move into one's own home. It's true that now you don't have to think twice about buying that extra pair of shoes; after all, there's no parent waiting at home to look at the package in your hand.

But one has to think about the electricity bill that is due next week, the telephone bill that now seems to be on an astronomical level, and other expenses that have to be paid. Money that has been earned after working hours seems to be forgotten. In Economics, we learn that a country grows only through investment. And investment is the direct result of savings.

Similarly, in the case of an individual, his or

her financial status grows through savings. Some of this savings can be invested in stocks and bonds. And since emergencies and accidents don't come with trailers before them, security regarding health and other insurance must be made.

Women in India have been financially dependent on men for a long time: first as their father's daughter, second as their husband's wife, and then as the mother of their children.

While this has saved them the worry of earning a living, it has also had its drawbacks. A wife abused by her husband is unable to leave him and support herself. Even after the divorce, she is at the mercy of her husband for the support of her children.

But with the changing times, the modern Indian woman knows how to make a living. The power of money no longer manipulates her life.

Living off others brings with it self-contempt and ridicule. Therefore, everyone should work towards financial independence.

Chapter 3: Begin Your Journey to Financial Freedom

To achieve financial stability and security in life, you have to plan and work hard over time. But to make things a little easier for you, here are the most important and time-tested features that could help you reach your financial goals.

Health is Wealth (take care of yourself)

This may seem immaterial, but it is very relevant. Good health ensures that not only do you have the physical and psychological vigor to meet and overcome the challenges of your life, but it also ensures that you will be there to savor the success of your dreams come true.

So get regular check-ups with your doctor, exercise regularly and maintain a healthy diet. And start early. The less careful you are now, the harder it will be to make up for it later.

Define your vision

Defining your vision of your work and life is crucial to your success. What do you want? Is it financial independence, to be your own boss, more security for your family, a solid launching pad for your children? Whatever it is, you must always be your vision in focus.

Reinforce the vision and your role in many ways, and in times of trouble look to it for guidance and comfort.

Invest your money wisely

Although your basic income should come from your current job, don't limit yourself to this. You should try to increase your income by investing your money wisely and profitably.

You could finance or start a business that you are passionate about; otherwise, you could invest in safe market options.

Save Your Money

A good way to build a solid financial foundation is to adopt the old savings mentality. Set aside a certain percentage of your income for savings on a regular basis, and set aside this money every month, every time you receive funds or get paid.

A convenient way to avoid compulsive buying and the trap of poor budget management is to always remember to pay your savings account first. This avoids unnecessary expenses and covers any contingencies that may arise. Although the interest on a savings account is lower than some other investments, setting aside savings is the safest option.

Power Trait-Spend your money wisely

Differentiate within your expenses and avoid strangers. Before any purchase, ask yourself if you really need it. Be true to yourself and your vision: "Do I really need that?" Only you can answer this question, but you must be true to yourself and your vision of financial independence.

Chapter 4: Tips to Ensure a Successful Financial Independence Plan

Even if you have determined a set of financial plans for yourself, whether it's market investing, real estate or retirement, you should try to coordinate these plans to maximize your earnings.

To help you achieve this, here are the 7 crucial steps for financial planning that will allow you to reach your goals, within the time frame you require, with tax benefits and minimal risk:

1) Emergency cash reserves: Always set aside 3-6 months of your salary in an account from which you can withdraw money in the short term without incurring any penalties. For any unexpected short-term expenses, try to avoid using credit cards and use this cash instead.

2) Risk management: Insurance is the safest form of risk management. Therefore, insure your car, your home and other important assets. You may also consider life insurance to help compensate for loss of income and pay off debts in the event of your death. While you are finalizing your insurance option, always choose the type of insurance that fits your needs, and work out the amount of coverage needed that is affordable to you.

3) Estate Planning: The basic features of an estate plan are a will and a durable power of attorney to provide for your medical and financial care. For larger estates, you may also require a living trust, marital trusts and charitable remainder trusts. These ensure that your assets are maintained and passed on to future generations.

4) Goal setting: This is the framework for coordinating your financial plan. Whenever you receive an investment offer, refer it to your overall financial goals. Ask yourself if it is conducive or productive "to", and fits "to", your goals. This commitment to your goals will help you stay focused over the long term.

5) Investments: You need to have a personalized asset investment plan to meet your objectives and keep the element of risk within the limits you consider acceptable. Without this, your investments will be subject to the vagaries of the economy rather than being driven by your requirements.

6) Retirement plans: Income to supplement your social security will come from defined contribution and benefit plans. During your working life, try to make as many annual contributions to these defined contribution plans as possible. These funds grow rapidly as a result of tax deferral, and since they are obtained directly from your salary, they are relatively painless.

7) Tax planning: This means taking advantage of all the possible tax deductions and tax-deferred plans that the law allows you, as well as using tax credits wherever you are eligible. A good tax plan can save you thousands of dollars in taxes.

If you feel that you cannot handle all of this on your own, seek the services of a paid financial advisor or financial coach to design a comprehensive plan according to your assets and needs.

Remember: Your financial security depends on properly coordinating these separate steps to create wealth.

Chapter 5: Working Toward Financial Independence

Many of us can talk about financial independence but the question is how many of us actually achieve it.

Very few percentages of us know how to make a sound plan and even fewer are able to be disciplined in executing the plan. Be careful and consider a money management program that will help you become financially independent.

Any type of financial planning begins with

proper money management. As you build your plan, be sure to work on two important aspects. First, address the issue of finding the fund that will support your plans and second, get the money planned in such a way that your goals are met.

This money will help you keep the opportunities that are important to you. You might be a little surprised to find that each of us has some sort of money management in place. There are several methods to carry out good money management. It is important that you have an organized approach to the plan and that you get the most out of the money. Focus on identifying your expenses so you know exactly how much to invest.

If you set a goal, it will give you a purpose for investing. Your plans may overlap, so be aware that your goals may overlap.

For example, your retirement plan may overlap with your investment and money management plan.

By now you should have realized that money management is important to future financial goals.

Please stick to a realistic money management plan. Consider how you would achieve the funds. Your goals should be specific. Prioritize your goals to make the path easier.

We are often fooled by a few pre-conceived notions such as living in the moment. We do not realize that there is a future waiting for us. It is important to have an organized approach.

If you don't have an organized approach you may find yourself in some kind of trouble.

You would have to pay extra taxes. You would expose yourself unnecessarily to financial risks.

Lack of funds for your children's higher education. Unsafe aging due to lack of planning

And just the opposite would be the case if an organized money management plan had been made at the right time.

The best result of proper money management is that you are able to meet both long and short-term expenses.

Chapter 6: New trends towards financial management

Economic insecurity is rapidly increasing in the hearts of people who, faced with the possibility of near bankruptcy due to the rising cost of living and the lack of availability of well-paying jobs, are focusing their attention on alternatives, in the marketplace, that will help them to provide for themselves and their families. Therefore, many are looking for any secondary source of income or planning security measures, to support them in case of financial emergency such as the loss of their job.

Others who are already suffering at the hands of social trends are desperately trying to make ends meet and are looking for an opportunity to restart their careers. There are also others who, following the market's guidelines, have managed to accumulate money and are trying to take advantage of their good run, hoping that their future years will be safe.

High Demand Services

That is why it is very important to choose the right type and the right profession. Whether it is a "sit at home" type company or a rigorous field company, nothing else ensures success except its market demand, even in the midst of a large-scale economic crisis.

Since today's world is completely governed by the powers of technology, especially the computer, having a job that keeps you in control of the evils of your job, such as identity theft and general computer problems, is a sure way to find success.

Just as with cars, people use them every day, but they don't know how to maintain and control them. So when things go wrong with computers, no matter how adverse the situation, they will be in high demand.

The best chances of success

So while anyone with a little luck and research can achieve success, people with experience in information services, sales and advertising, or those who are amateurs have a guaranteed chance of success.

The possibilities are even more favorable for small business sole proprietors, since they can use these products on their website to make more money.

Where to look

If you are looking for a healthy victory, then the best option for you is to join hands in partnership with a solid and reputable company, which will help you maximize your profits and help you on your way to a safe and economic future. But before you partner, analyze the company's reimbursement plans and support systems so you can get the best and safest deal from this company.

Chapter 7: Money Matters

With the rapid rise in cost and standard of living, bankruptcy is becoming a fairly common phenomenon - loans, credit card fees, honoraria, etc. - the list goes on. If you don't know how to handle your finances and the stress builds up, you may start to feel that filing for bankruptcy is the only way out.

It is important to understand that this should be your last resort. Before that, you should try counseling and debit card management services and better budget management.

You can also check out debt settlement plans and see if they work for you. Get a counselor to help you find things. But remember that a debt settlement plan will only give you a break. It won't be real and it will make all your problems go away.

You should find a counselor with enough experience. Getting references from people you know is a good idea. The debt counselor will negotiate with your lenders to lower your fees and interest rates.

Second, he or she will also help you consolidate all your debts into one amount. That way, you don't have to worry about managing your payments. You will only have to pay one amount due. He/she will help you get your paperwork and applications in order. All this can help you regain your financial position in a relatively short period of time.

Of course, there are some minimum requirements to get into the program. If you qualify for the program, your monthly budget will be crossed out and a required amount of money will be set aside for your payments. Systematizing things will help you get back on track.

If you're tired of paying the bills that are piling up in front of your face, it's time to rethink your life a little. Enrolling in the above program is a good first step. It will give you a new and positive direction in your life.

It's crucial to managing your loans properly and if you can't do it yourself you shouldn't hesitate to ask for help. It's important to do these things right, if you don't want to jeopardize everything you care about.

Money management is a very important skill. One needs to be taught the importance of saving money and planning a budget from the beginning of life. Be careful with the steps before you have to learn these lessons the hard way.

But if you do get into trouble, don't think twice about hiring the help of a debt counselor. They will give you a plan for your specific, personalized needs. Choose your plan wisely.

One of the most popular plans can get you back on your feet, financially, in as little as five years.

But remember, you have to want to get out of trouble and stay out of it.

You have to have a strong determination to keep your finances in order and not splurge on things you can't afford in the end.

If you do get a second chance at your financial life, don't waste it. Learn to be prudent in money matters before it's too late.

Chapter 8: Distinguishing Between Wants and Needs in Life to Achieve Financial Freedom

Financial freedom and security come from regulating your needs and wants wisely.

Money offers security, but it also takes away your security if it is spent on the wrong things. To deal with this paradox, it is necessary to understand and follow the basic differences between needs and wants in life.

It is important to handle money in such a

way that you do not have to beg and borrow from someone else when there is a shortage of it. These situations can be avoided if you can avoid certain luxuries in life and instead concentrate on saving money to meet life's basic needs.

If you don't have enough money to lead a normal and comfortable life, you will end up leading an inhibited and unpleasant life. You will also end up doing the wrong job and this will make you unhappy and unsatisfied. If there is no security in your life, you will also become less active in your life. It will also prevent you from doing what you really want to do in life, limiting your options and restricting your lifestyle.

The luxuries in life can be largely avoided as long as you have the basic needs in place.

Luxuries are add-ons and can wait for some time as long as we have enough money in our pockets.

This may seem restrictive to many people. They might even argue that it doesn't make sense to wait for a fantastic future when you have money to satisfy all your needs and desires. First of all, you must understand that money cannot guarantee you anything in life.

Money is not an end in itself. It is up to each person to handle money wisely to satisfy his or her ends. You must be strict with your money and spend it only on things you cannot do without.

This logic applies not only to adults, but also to students and children. The value of money must be perceived at a very young age so that your whole world does not revolve around making money. There are other things in life that are not just money.

If you know exactly what you want and what you want to become in life, you can work to get it and get things out of there. Once you are financially secure and independent you can live life the way you want.

This does not mean that you live a luxurious life spending money on unwanted things. By taking into account the difference between desires and goals, you can lead a full and uninhibited life.

Chapter 9: Organizing Your Debt for Financial Freedom

The latest data released by the Federal Reserve, the organization that tracks and records all monetary affairs in the United States, reveals that Americans owe more than two trillion dollars on their credit cards and that the total debt of every person in the country amounts to more than seven thousand dollars.

These staggering figures for credit card debt in the U.S. are bound to affect everyone. So what are the solutions available? You could start by following the suggestions below, which will help you effectively manage your financial responsibilities: Organize your outstanding debt - Start by taking stock of any and all revolving obligations you have. This would include all your credit and debit cards. Tabulate and record your liabilities based on payment schedules, bills, etc. Accounting for applicable interest rates calculates the exact amount you owe.

It is important to know the interest rate on your monthly debts, as this is the ongoing cost you incur against ongoing debt each month. Therefore, it is beneficial to you if you can pay off the loan by charging the highest interest rate as soon as possible.

So while you're making payments, try to send as much as possible to the lender with the highest rate, even if it means you're left with only the minimum payments due on the rest. This way, once the debt with the highest interest has been paid off, you can follow the same policy for the loan with the next highest interest rate.

Negotiate for lower interest rates - try to maintain an immaculate payment history and then call or meet with your lenders and ask them to lower your interest rate. Because it is expensive for lenders to find new customers, if your creditworthiness is proven, they will always try to keep you. Therefore, most lenders will owe customers in good standing to enjoy the reduced rates. However, once they agree to lower your rate, be sure to pay your bills on time; otherwise, they may withdraw the facility and raise the applicable interest rate again.

Use cash when you can - Because it is much easier to use a card than to carry cash or write checks, most of us get into the habit of using cards even if they attract fees. So try to cultivate the habit of writing a check and paying cash rather than instinctively using the credit card.

Always keep in mind that a credit card purchase is not a gift but a loan. So be well advised when using the card: prefer not to use the card at all if you cannot afford the responsibility.

Remember that it is better not to spend on everything than to spend so much that it starts to hurt you.

If you can organize your finances, minimize

your costs and make them proportional to your earnings, you will be sure to put your tour finances in order and avoid any problems in the future. If you put your mind to it, financial freedom is not such hard work, and it is well worth all the effort.

Chapter 10: Six Ways to Teach Children about Money and Financial Markets

If you plan to teach your child to learn how to manage money, then the best way to do so is to start paying off your debts soon. When money matters, kids need to have a first-hand experience. If they do, they will understand what it takes to make the exchange.

If your child wants something from you, instead of buying it, give her the money. You must realize that it is important for your child to know how to handle money.

When a child reaches a certain age, you should realize his or her inclinations and let the child handle the money on his or her own. Let the child buy his or her own basic needs, such as school supplies. But make sure the child knows his or her limitations. As a caregiver you should keep a sharp eye on his activities.

The next step would be for you as a guardian to establish a budget for your children. Children, no matter how young, have the ability to keep a notebook in which they can write down the money they have and the money they have spent. Make sure your children know their future goals and it's your duty to make sure they achieve them.

As your child grows and matures, open a savings account for them - you'll be surprised how great this can be! It's very satisfying to see compound interest add up. Make an extra effort and show your child by graphing how the account grows. And show him that if he keeps doing it, what the count will be like after a few years.

Have her play a major role while you make a major purchase, such as a dishwasher or a car. Let him know that the amount of research that goes into a new purchase The process of discount comparison and negotiation is important and you will learn this. Make sure your child is with you on the actual day of the purchase.

Your children will be privileged if they have a gift for the business world. Increase the value of the stock and over time if they start owning some stock it could improve. The rise and fall of prices would be interesting for young investors. So we owe them full freedom.

Chapter 11: Financial Independence for seniors

The government-initiated reverse mortgage program has been a blessing to many seniors. The plan, which allows people aged 62 and over to exchange a portion of their home's equity for tax-free money and does not have to be repaid while they are alive, makes it convenient for them to lead full and unyielding lives even when most of the country is plagued by rising expenses in all spheres of life.

Moreover, the effects of such expenses are multiplied when it comes to the older generation, because they have to deal not only with property taxes, but also with general expenses such as health and household.

Thus, this ends up making the lives of the elderly anything but relaxed and peaceful.

Increasingly high land taxes are becoming a burden to these elderly people. It is especially problematic for retired professionals for whom two months of savings equals a small amount of tax due.

This tax problem is becoming the cause of many of them leaving their homes in their 20s and 30s because of inability to pay. This is where Kaye Financial Corporation, one of Michigan's leading mortgage companies, has been of great help to these seniors.

In light of the fact that most of these people are forced to survive on a certain amount of given income, they are forced to compromise on important factors in their lives to meet the rents on the homes.

But now with this new reverse mortgage scheme, they can use the extra money to live a full life, without worrying about how to get resources to survive, even after retirement.

This is especially beneficial because the money is provided according to the person's needs. It can be sent in full in a massive amount, once a month, or in small amounts when needed.

Thus, it becomes advantageous for everyone according to their needs.

Also, since most loans are off-limits to seniors, reverse lending comes as reassuring news to them, since there are no income, health, or age requirements attached to applying for it.

Thus, such schemes provide older people with a sense of well-being, freedom and security.

In addition, they can use the money from this reverse mortgage plan to pay taxes, rent, bills, and other expenses such as the mortgage, so they can live a life without commitments.

So it can be said that the reverse mortgage plan is then the best thing that could have happened to these senior citizens, as they will now be able to continue living their lives to the fullest extent of their wishes.

Chapter 12: Financial Independence and Retirement Planning

Financial independence is essential for all of us after retirement. We all want a comfortable and relaxed life in our old age. Unfortunately, most of us cannot have the kind of life we wanted after leaving work, simply because of lack of money.

In several situations, people have to continue working even after retirement, simply to meet basic needs. The unhappy circumstance could have been different with a certain amount of careful and easy preparation and investment.

These points can allow you to have the financial independence and life you wanted at a later age.

1. The position you aspire to in the end - Remember that the vital section of any aging plan is figuring out the position you want in the latter part of life. Most of us have no idea what life we want in old age, and so we jump into old age schemes without a proper mental goal set in our mind.

2. Wish List - Just as you don't drive a car without having a clue where you want to go, don't plan without thinking. When you take any retirement plan, list all the ones you wish to have after you leave work. List the type of residence you want, the type of car you want, the type of life you want and so on. Don't miss anything. Write down everything down to the last detail.

3. Keep the sheet of paper somewhere more accessible. That way you can see it as much as possible. This process will gradually set the goals you have for retirement and old age on your mental levels. Then, you will gradually form concepts for achieving those goals simply by seeing them and possessing them mentally.

4. Calculate the money needed for the goals - Calculate the amount of funding needed to make the goals a reality. Then look for the assets and investment policies, which can get you there. I will suggest that you get to know all the retirement plans and plans for old age. Then you will be in complete control of the future.

Most of us leave the various aspects of our retirement plans to a money management corporation. But you handle it yourself. Check out the books that deal with investment policies and how to make money.

These points can help you achieve a financially free life in your later years.

Chapter 13: Freedom Has a Price

For anyone who is planning, or going, to start a home-based business, there are some basic conditions and warnings that come in small print, and about which potential recruiters never say much. But it is imperative that you pay due attention to these basic truths.

First, remember that you will always have to make some sacrifices. You will have to spend money, time, and energy to get any business off the ground. Most recruiters misrepresent the opportunity when they insist that anyone can do it, not to mention the high failure rate.

This means you'll have to sacrifice some or most of the time you would otherwise spend doing the things you enjoy or in the company of friends and family. This will undoubtedly lead to stress and resentment and you need to be prepared in advance to handle the consequences.

In addition, you will need the extra energy, beyond your normal quota for your regular job, family and home, to do the things necessary for your business. So you need to tap into your extra reserves: develop your drive to succeed and stay motivated by telling yourself that it will all be worth it in the long run.

As for the financial sacrifices, there are ways to gradually absorb the burden or even eliminate it completely, but in advance, you need to set aside some money to get things going.

The strategy is to be able to see these sacrifices as something positive and productive. So you have to be optimistic and consider them as investments for your future and your independence.

Consider the advantages of prudence and strength: don't be discouraged by initial failures, but learn from them. You can make your sacrifices and failures the foundation of your success.

Your success is what you make and give to yourself. You can think of it as your reward, as something that has already been done in your name, but your part is to deserve it, to make it yours. So go out there and look for your success that is waiting for you to achieve it. There will be times when you will be tested, but you will have to grit your teeth, clench your fists and squeeze. At times like these, just close your mind to all the negative elements, and press to keep your goal and your vision in mind. This is all much easier said than done, but it is also the long, hard road to success.

Chapter 14: Setting Goals for Financial Independence

The first step you should take while managing your money is to have a financial goal. The New Year is an ideal time to help you make some important decisions. It's a time to review your financial goals. Your goals will help you move forward with your finances.

You should have something to work for every day. You should have a planned budget and use these goals you have set as your roadmap. These financial goals help motivate you and encourage you to save.

Without a proper plan it is difficult to get anywhere, so it is important to be well directed.

If you don't have a financial goal, you will never be able to achieve financial independence. You need to put your finger on the things you need to achieve. Make a list of the things you want. Your list can start with the first step of being debt-free; you can continue to owe by starting a retirement account, saving enough to sponsor a home for yourself and other basic needs.

Don't let this entire stop you from writing down everything you want and want to include in your financial planning. In case you're looking for new furniture or a trip to Europe, include that too.

These are money goals that are achievable. Be sure to prioritize your wishes. You must realize that getting out of debt is of the utmost urgency, whereas a tour of Europe can wait.

There are certain goals that we work on constantly, and there are some that wait for certain goals to be met before they can be executed. It is important to set time constraints for the fulfilment of the objectives.

Take for example that there may be about 25 years before you retire, so you would want to be debt-free in about 6 years. Work wisely on your goals. Remember that you are always open to changing them.

Your next step would be to break down your goals into short-term goals. When we break a big task into small steps, it helps us accomplish them better. It makes the task easier. Let's see how this would work to get us out of debt. We need to do one task at a time.

Success and prosperity!

Visit our author page on Amazon and get more **MENTES LIBRES!**

http://amazon.com/author/menteslibres

If you wish, you can leave a comment on this book by clicking on the following link so that we can continue to grow! Thank you very much for your purchase!

https://www.amazon.com/dp/B08545RX26

www.ingramcontent.com/pod-product-compliance
Lightning Source LLC
Chambersburg PA
CBHW050257220526
45465CB00002B/721